DISCOVERING THE UNITED STATES

Puerto Rico

BY ANNETTE M. CLAYTON

Kids Core

An Imprint of Abdo Publishing
abdobooks.com

abdobooks.com

Printed in China.
052024
092024

Cover Photo: Martin Wheeler/Alamy
Interior Photos: Universal History Archive/Universal Images Group/Getty Images, 4–5; W. Marissen/iStockphoto, 7 (top left); E. Rojas/Shutterstock Images, 7 (top right); Shutterstock Images, 7 (bottom left), 7 (bottom right), 8, 14, 23; Dennis van de Water/Shutterstock Images, 10, 28 (bottom right); Van der Meer Marica/Arterra Picture Library/Alamy, 12–13; Gabriele Holtermann/Sipa USA/AP Images, 17; Holly Mazour/Shutterstock Images, 18; iStockphoto, 20–21, 28 (bottom left); Colac Catalin/Shutterstock Images, 24; Jeremy A. Casado/Shutterstock Images, 25; Bryan Mullennix World View/Alamy, 26; Chad Zuber/Shutterstock Images, 28 (top left); Steve Heap/Shutterstock Images, 28 (top right); Red Line Editorial, 29 (top), 29 (bottom)

Editor: Haley Williams
Series Designer: Katharine Hale

Library of Congress Control Number: 2023949470

Publisher's Cataloging-in-Publication Data

Names: Clayton, Annette M., author.
Title: Puerto Rico / by Annette M. Clayton
Description: Minneapolis, Minnesota: Abdo Publishing, 2025 | Series: Discovering the United States | Includes online resources and index.
Identifiers: ISBN 9781098294090 (lib. bdg.) | ISBN 9798384913368 (ebook)
Subjects: LCSH: U.S. states--Juvenile literature. | Puerto Rico--History--Juvenile literature. | Puerto Rico--Relations--United States--Juvenile literature. | Physical geography--United States--Juvenile literature.
Classification: DDC 973--dc23

All population data taken from:
"Estimates of Population by Sex, Race, and Hispanic Origin: April 1, 2020 to July 1, 2022." *US Census Bureau, Population Division*, June 2023, census.gov.

CONTENTS

CHAPTER 1
Becoming a US Territory 4

CHAPTER 2
The People of Puerto Rico 12

CHAPTER 3
Places in Puerto Rico 20

Territory Map 28
Glossary 30
Online Resources 31
Learn More 31
Index 32
About the Author 32

On May 12, 1898, the United States attacked a fort in San Juan, Puerto Rico, that was being used as a Spanish military base.

CHAPTER 1

Becoming a US Territory

It was the late 1800s. The island of Puerto Rico was a **colony** of Spain. The island was used as a military base. Puerto Ricans wanted independence from Spanish rule. But they were not able to break free from Spain's control.

In 1898, the United States and Spain fought in the Spanish-American War. The United States wanted to stop Spain's rule in Puerto Rico and on the island of Cuba. After several months of fighting, Spain lost the war. It **ceded** Puerto Rico to the United States. The island became a US **territory**. Then in 1917, Puerto Ricans were given US citizenship.

Today, Puerto Rico is a self-governed island. But it is still considered part of the United States. Many people visit Puerto Rico every year to see everything the island has to offer.

Puerto Rico's Land

Puerto Rico is one of 14 US territories. It is located in the Caribbean Sea. The island is more than

Puerto Rico Facts

DATE OF BECOMING US TERRITORY
December 10, 1898

CAPITAL
San Juan

POPULATION
3,221,789

AREA
5,325 square miles (13,792 sq km)

OFFICIAL BIRD

Spindalis

OFFICIAL TREE

Ceiba

OFFICIAL FLOWER

Flor de Maga

OFFICIAL DISH

Arroz con gandules

Each US state and territory has a different population, size, and capital city. They also have official symbols.

1,000 miles (1,610 km) from the United States. Puerto Rico is an archipelago. This means it is made up of one main island and more than a hundred smaller islands. The main island of Puerto Rico is 100 miles (161 km) long.

Puerto Rico is known for having many beautiful beaches along its coasts.

It is 35 miles (56 km) wide. Two of Puerto Rico's smaller islands are Vieques and Culebra.

Puerto Rico has varied landscapes. About 60 percent of the island is covered by mountains. The tallest mountain is Cerro de Punta. It is about 4,390 feet (1,338 m) tall. The island also has lowlands and tropical rainforests. In addition, there are several beaches along the coast.

Fruit trees grow year-round in Puerto Rico. They include mango, passion fruit, banana, and citrus trees. Many kinds of animals can be found on the island as well. The coqui is the most famous animal in Puerto Rico. It is a frog about 1 to 2 inches (2.5–5 cm) long. Coquis have a loud call that sounds like their name, *co-kee*.

Hurricane Maria

In 2017, Hurricane Maria tore through Puerto Rico. It brought heavy rains and wind speeds of 100 miles per hour (160 km/h). The storm caused lots of damage. Many people were left without electricity and running water for months. More than 300,000 homes on the island were destroyed.

Some parts of El Yunque National Forest can receive more than 200 inches (510 cm) of rainfall a year.

Puerto Rico's Climate

Puerto Rico has a tropical climate. The weather is usually sunny, warm, and **humid**. The southern part of the island is warmer than the north. Central Puerto Rico is often cooler because of the mountains.

The island experiences a lot of rain. Hurricanes are also common. This is due to the island's location in the Caribbean. Hurricanes often occur between August and October.

Explore Online

Visit the website below. Does it give any new information about Puerto Rico that wasn't in Chapter One?

Puerto Rico

abdocorelibrary.com/discovering-puerto-rico

A sculpture honoring a former Taíno chief is carved into the side of a cliff in the town of Isabela.

The People of Puerto Rico

The Taíno were the first people of Puerto Rico. They arrived in Puerto Rico around 400 BCE. The Taíno came from other Caribbean islands. They grew corn, beans, and a potato-like vegetable called yuca. They also fished off the island's coasts.

The three red stripes and sides of the triangle on Puerto Rico's flag represent the island's three branches of government.

In 1493, European explorer Christopher Columbus landed on the island. He claimed it for Spain. Spanish **colonists** were harsh to the Taíno people. Many Taíno were taken as slaves or were killed. Others died from disease. In 1517, the Spanish brought enslaved people from West Africa to Puerto Rico. Those enslaved were forced to work in gold mines and on farms.

In 2022, more than 3.2 million people lived in Puerto Rico. About 99 percent of the population was Hispanic or Latino. Black people made up 10 percent of the population. And less than 1 percent of Puerto Ricans were white.

Culture

Spanish and English are the official languages of Puerto Rico. But the island is influenced by many different cultures. This includes influences from Spain, West Africa, the Taíno, and the United States.

The island's cultural traditions show up in its popular dishes. Enslaved African people brought a type of banana called a plantain to Puerto Rico. Plantains are still used in many dishes. Mofongo is made of plantains mashed with garlic and pork skin. The dish is usually fried.

Roberto Clemente

Baseball is the most popular sport in Puerto Rico. Roberto Clemente was a famous baseball player from the island. He played for the Pittsburgh Pirates from 1955 to 1972. Today, Major League Baseball gives out the Roberto Clemente Award each year. The award goes to a player who shows strong character and who is involved in the community.

National Puerto Rican Day celebrates the people and culture of Puerto Rico. A huge parade is held in New York City every June.

Another popular dish in Puerto Rico is pernil. Pernil is roasted pork flavored with spices. It is often eaten around the holidays.

Many Puerto Ricans enjoy dancing and music. Bomba is a popular music style and dance. It was created by enslaved African people. They danced to the beat of drums to express themselves. Today, many Puerto Ricans continue dancing to and playing bomba music. They do so to honor their **ancestors**.

Several kinds of crops are produced in Puerto Rico, including sugarcane, plantains, and coffee, *pictured*.

Industry

Puerto Rico has several major industries. The **pharmaceutical** industry employs many Puerto Ricans. Workers make lifesaving medicines. Tourism is another important industry. Nearly 3 million people visit the island every year. Many Puerto Ricans have jobs in hotels, restaurants, and retail.

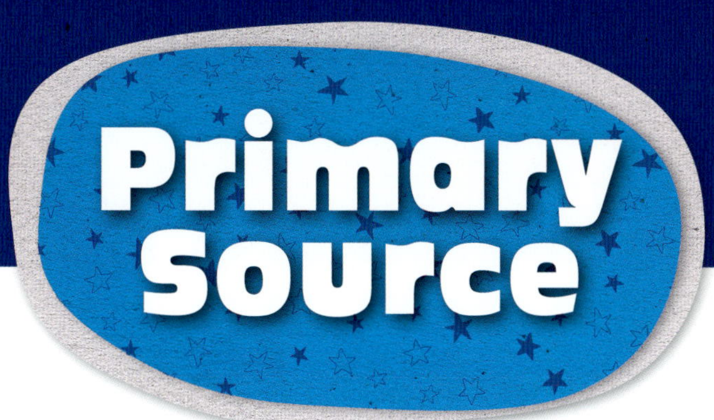

Manuel Ayala is a bomba musician from Puerto Rico. He spoke about the importance of bomba in Puerto Rican culture:

> More than just a genre of music, bomba for us is the foundation of which all our cultural expressions evolved from. Puerto Rico is bomba.

Source: "Puerto Rico Is Bomba." *YouTube*, uploaded by Discover Puerto Rico, 27 Apr. 2020, youtube.com. Accessed 6 Nov. 2023.

What's the Big Idea?

Read this quote carefully. What is its main idea? Explain how the main idea is supported by details.

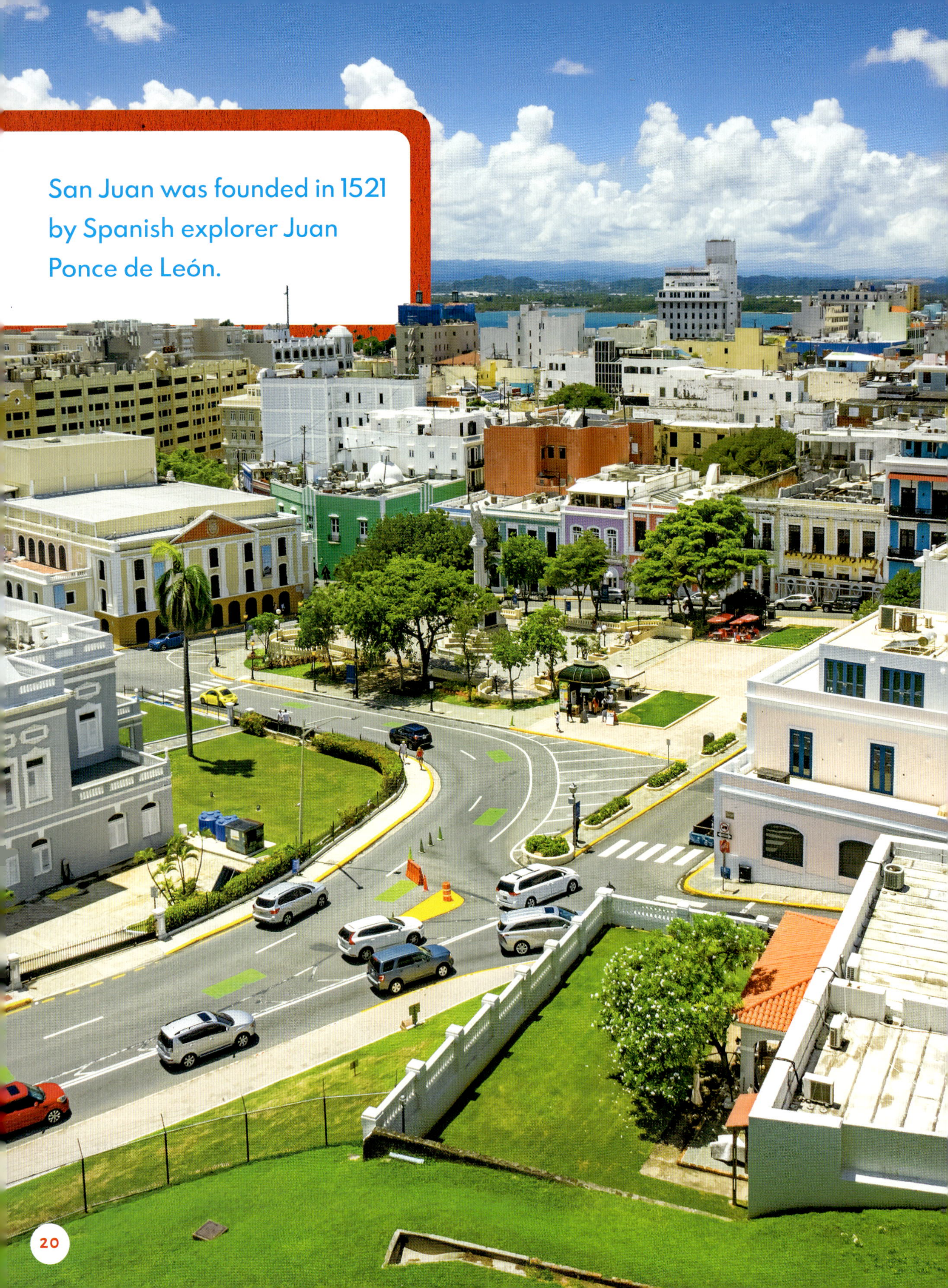

San Juan was founded in 1521 by Spanish explorer Juan Ponce de León.

Places in Puerto Rico

San Juan is Puerto Rico's capital. It is the most **populated** city on the island. Old San Juan is a district within the capital. It is a popular place to visit. People can shop, eat, and tour the area. Other cities on the island include Bayamón and Carolina.

Parks and Landmarks

Puerto Rico has many parks and landmarks. El Yunque National Forest is the only tropical rainforest in the US National Forest System. The forest covers 28,516 acres (11,540 ha) of land. Many animals can be found there. This includes

Vieques National Wildlife Refuge

Vieques National Wildlife Refuge on the island of Vieques is the largest national wildlife refuge in the Caribbean. A refuge is a protected place for animals. This refuge covers more than 17,770 acres (7,190 ha) on Vieques. Many endangered animals live there. This includes four species of sea turtles and the brown pelican.

La Coca waterfall is a popular site to visit in El Yunque National Forest.

the Puerto Rican parrot and the coqui. People visit the forest to hike, go zip-lining, and see waterfalls.

Castillo San Felipe del Morro is part of the San Juan National Historic Site, which protects several important sites in San Juan.

Castillo San Felipe del Morro is a fort overlooking the San Juan Bay. It is also called El Morro. Construction of the fort began in 1539. But it wasn't completed until 1790. The fort was

Brown pelicans are commonly seen at La Guancha Boardwalk.

used to protect Puerto Rico from invaders by sea. Today, visitors can tour El Morro and learn about its history. They can also see amazing ocean views from the fort.

La Guancha Boardwalk in Ponce is another popular destination. Visitors can swim in the ocean. They can try delicious food as they walk along the boardwalk. People can also buy seeds to feed the birds and fish in the area.

Parque de Bombas was used as Ponce's fire station for more than 100 years before it closed in 1990.

Parque de Bombas is a famous building in Ponce. The old fire station is known for its bright colors. People can visit the museum there that honors the town's firefighters. On the island of Vieques, many people enjoy visiting

Mosquito Bay. Tiny creatures make the bay's water glow in the dark. Kayaking through the glowing water is a popular activity.

Puerto Rico is an amazing island. It has sunny beaches and colorful cities. People can hike through the rainforest and splash in the ocean. They can also enjoy live music on the streets. There are so many things to experience in Puerto Rico.

Further Evidence

Look at the website below. Does it give any new evidence to support what you learned in Chapter Three?

El Yunque: Wildlife Species

abdocorelibrary.com/discovering-puerto-rico

Territory Map

Flamenco Beach

Los Morillos Lighthouse

San Juan

El Yunque National Forest

Puerto Rico: The Island of Enchantment

Glossary

ancestors
the people from whom a person is descended and who lived many generations ago

ceded
gave up control

colonists
people who have moved to and taken control of an area

colony
an area that is controlled by another country

humid
describing air that has a lot of moisture

pharmaceutical
related to the development and sale of medicines

populated
settled or lived in

territory
a particular area of land that belongs to and is governed by a country

Online Resources

To learn more about Puerto Rico, visit our free resource websites below.

Visit **abdocorelibrary.com** or scan this QR code for free Common Core resources for teachers and students, including vetted activities, multimedia, and booklinks, for deeper subject comprehension.

Visit **abdobooklinks.com** or scan this QR code for free additional online weblinks for further learning. These links are routinely monitored and updated to provide the most current information available.

Learn More

Murray, Julie. *Animals of the Rain Forest.* Abdo, 2023.

Romo Edelman, Claudia. *Roberto Clemente.* Roaring Brook, 2022.

Tieck, Sarah. *Puerto Rico.* Abdo, 2020.

Index

bomba, 17, 19

Cerro de Punta, 8
Clemente, Roberto, 16
climate, 11
coquis, 9, 23
Culebra, 8

dishes, 7, 16–17

El Morro, 24–25
El Yunque National Forest, 22–23, 27

Hurricane Maria, 9

industries, 18

Ponce, 25–26
population, 7, 15, 21

San Juan, 7, 21
Spanish-American War, 6

Taíno peoples, 13–15

Vieques, 8, 22, 26

About the Author

Annette M. Clayton is an author with Puerto Rican roots. She has written more than 20 books for children. When she's not writing, you can find her hiking on the Appalachian Trail. Annette resides in Maryland with her husband and twin daughters.